Makerspace Cardboard Challenge!

CARDBOARD ROCKET CHALLENGE!

Sue Gagliardi

DiscoverRoo
An Imprint of Pop!
popbooksonline.com

abdobooks.com

Published by Pop!, a division of ABDO, PO Box 398166, Minneapolis, Minnesota 55439. Copyright © 2021 by POP, LLC. International copyrights reserved in all countries. No part of this book may be reproduced in any form without written permission from the publisher. Pop!™ is a trademark and logo of POP, LLC.

Printed in the United States of America, North Mankato, Minnesota.

052020
092020

THIS BOOK CONTAINS RECYCLED MATERIALS

Cover Photos: ian nolan/Alamy, top left; Shutterstock Images, top right, bottom
Interior Photos: ian nolan/Alamy, 1 (top left); Shutterstock Images, 1 (top right), 1 (bottom), 27; NASA, 5, 6, 7, 8–9, 11, 12, 13, 14, 15, 16, 17, 29, 30, 31; iStockphoto, 19, 20, 21, 28; LightField Studios Inc./Alamy, 22; Photo Yom Lam/Alamy, 23, 24, 25 (top), 25 (bottom)

Editor: Meg Gaertner
Series Designer: Jake Slavik

Library of Congress Control Number: 2019955014
Publisher's Cataloging-in-Publication Data
Names: Gagliardi, Sue, author.
Title: Cardboard rocket challenge! / by Sue Gagliardi
Description: Minneapolis, Minnesota : POP!, 2021 | Series: Makerspace cardboard challenge! | Includes online resources and index.
Identifiers: ISBN 9781532167942 (lib. bdg.) | ISBN 9781644944547 (pbk.) | ISBN 9781532169045 (ebook)
Subjects: LCSH: Cardboard art--Juvenile literature. | Crafts (Handicrafts)--Juvenile literature. | Creative thinking in children--Juvenile literature. | Maker spaces--Juvenile literature.
Classification: DDC 745.54--dc23

WELCOME TO DiscoverRoo!

Pop open this book and you'll find QR codes loaded with information, so you can learn even more!

Scan this code* and others like it while you read, or visit the website below to make this book pop!

popbooksonline.com/rocket-challenge

*Scanning QR codes requires a web-enabled smart device with a QR code reader app and a camera.

TABLE OF CONTENTS

CHAPTER 1
In the Real World 4

CHAPTER 2
How Rockets Work 10

CHAPTER 3
Rocket Challenge. 18

CHAPTER 4
Improving Your Design. 26

Making Connections. 30
Glossary 31
Index. 32
Online Resources 32

CHAPTER 1
IN THE REAL WORLD

Rockets are machines that **launch** spacecraft into space. Some rockets take people and supplies into **orbit**. Other rockets sent shuttles beyond Earth's **atmosphere**. Rockets travel great

WATCH A VIDEO HERE!

Between 1981 and 2011, NASA's space shuttle program sent shuttles into space on 135 missions.

distances. They reach great speeds.

Rockets make space travel possible.

Scientists use rockets to study the planets. For example, rockets send **probes** into space. Probes fly by planets and moons. Probes take pictures and send them back to Earth.

Rockets sent robots to Mars. The robots collect information about the planet. They send the information back to Earth.

Satellites take pictures from space. They help people see deeper into space.

Rockets also launch **satellites**. The satellites orbit Earth. They take pictures of Earth. People use the pictures to predict the weather. Satellites also send phone and TV signals around Earth. They make communication easy.

A rocket launch creates a lot of fire and smoke.

To enter orbit, spacecraft must move against Earth's **gravity**. So, rockets create a huge amount of force. This force helps launch the spacecraft. The force is called thrust. A rocket's design helps it create thrust.

THINK ABOUT IT

What do you think would happen if a spacecraft could not move up against Earth's gravity?

CHAPTER 2
HOW ROCKETS WORK

Rocket engines burn **fuel** to create thrust. They turn the fuel into a hot gas. The engines push the hot gas downward. The force of this movement pushes the rocket upward.

LEARN MORE HERE!

Unlike airplane engines, rocket engines are designed to work in space, where there is no air.

Ares I is a two-stage rocket. It weighs 2 million pounds (907,000 kg). Engineers planned to use it to carry astronauts into Earth orbit.

Many rockets are divided into stages. Each stage has one or more engines. The first stage of a rocket burns fuel first. It lifts the rocket miles above Earth. The rocket gets lighter as it burns fuel.

Engineers planned to use the two-stage Ares V rocket to carry astronauts and supplies to the moon.

Once it runs out of fuel, the first stage separates from the rocket. It falls down to Earth. Meanwhile, the second-stage engine begins to burn its own fuel. It carries the rocket into Earth **orbit**.

Astronaut Buzz Aldrin stands on the surface of the moon in 1969.

PARTS OF A SATURN V ROCKET

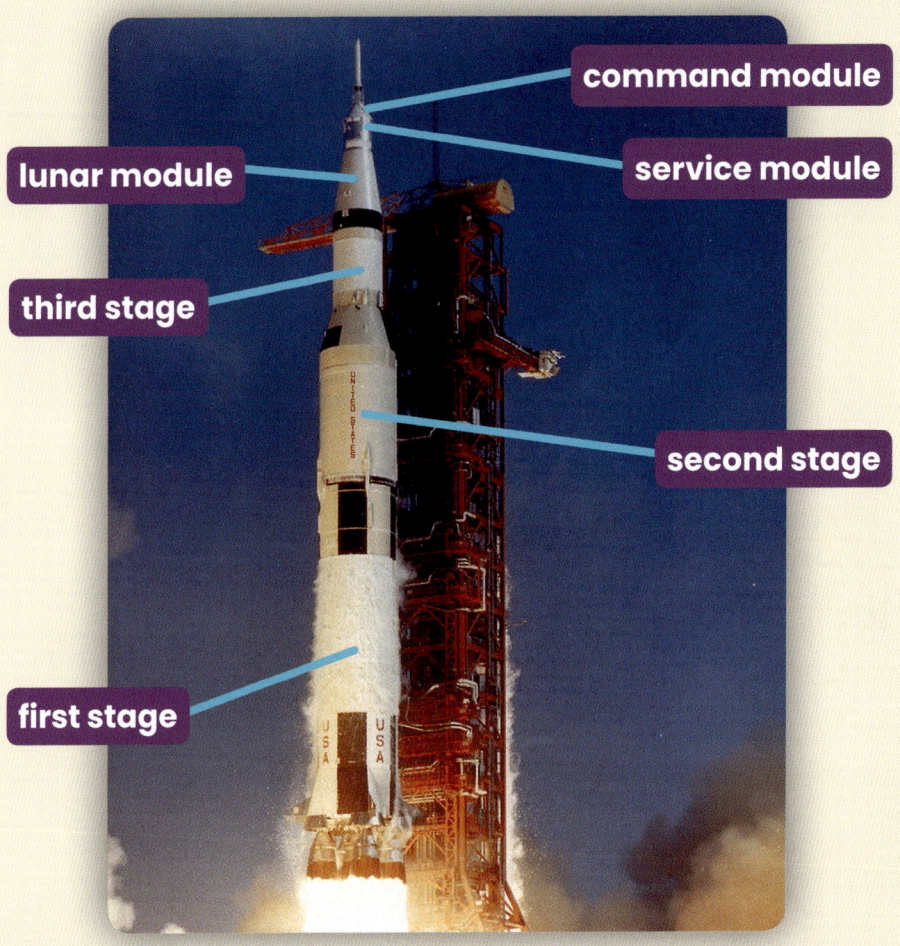

Saturn V was a three-stage rocket that took US astronauts to the moon in 1969. Astronauts sat in the command module during their journey to and from the moon. The service module carried oxygen and water for the astronauts. The lunar module is the vehicle that took astronauts down to the moon's surface.

Rockets must be large enough to carry the fuel required for the journey.

Engineers make rockets as light as possible. But the rockets must also be strong. They must withstand the great force created during a **launch**. So, engineers choose materials that are strong but also lightweight.

THINK ABOUT IT
Why might engineers want to make rockets as light as possible?

The first stage of the Space Launch System is 212 feet (65 m) long.

CHAPTER 3
ROCKET CHALLENGE

Challenge yourself to build a rocket. Draw a design for your rocket. Build your rocket out of cardboard and other materials. Then test your design.

COMPLETE AN ACTIVITY HERE!

This boy is connecting pieces of cardboard with tape.

THINK ABOUT IT

How could you test your cardboard rocket? How would you decide if the design works well?

Many rockets have thin, pointed wings.

Rockets push air out of the way as they fly through Earth's **atmosphere**. The air pushes back with a force called drag. Drag slows rockets down. Engineers

design rockets carefully. They choose

shapes that lower the force of drag.

This rocket has three levels, just like the stages of some real rockets.

For example, real rockets are narrow and tube-shaped. They also have nose cones. These pointed or curved shapes go at the front of rockets. The air flows around the nose cones. This design helps rockets fly faster and farther. What materials could you use to make a nose cone? What shape will your rocket have?

This cardboard rocket has a nose cone.

SUPPLY LIST

- packing boxes
- ruler
- cardboard egg cartons
- cereal boxes

tape or glue

paper towel tubes

sketch pad or paper for planning

scissors   index cards   paper clips

paint, markers, or crayons

CHAPTER 4
IMPROVING YOUR DESIGN

Try different designs for your rocket. See how they fly. How do different shapes move through the air? How do different sizes and materials affect the rocket's flights?

LEARN MORE HERE!

This boy made his rocket big enough to stand inside.

THINK ABOUT IT

Why might it be helpful to try different designs for your rocket?

This boy added red string to the end of his rocket. The red string looks like fire coming out of the rocket's engines.

Real rockets have engines that burn **fuel** and create thrust. Thrust helps rockets move upward against Earth's

gravity. Thrust also helps rockets withstand drag. How could you make your rocket fly?

SPACE LAUNCH SYSTEM

The Space **Launch** System (SLS) is a very powerful rocket. It can carry heavy loads into space. Engineers designed it to send astronauts to the moon. The SLS must create a lot of thrust to escape Earth **orbit**. In order to create thrust, it has two solid rocket boosters. It also has four engines at its back end. The SLS can hold 730,000 gallons (2.8 million L) of fuel.

Engineers look at a model of the Space Launch System.

MAKING CONNECTIONS

TEXT-TO-SELF

Would you want to travel to space? Why or why not?

TEXT-TO-TEXT

Have you read other books about rockets? What did you learn?

TEXT-TO-WORLD

Scientists use rockets to learn about space. Why do you think people want to know about outer space?

GLOSSARY

atmosphere – the layers of gases that surround a planet.

fuel – a material that is burned to create force.

gravity – a force that pulls objects toward Earth's center.

launch – to send something into the air.

orbit – a curved path that a spacecraft or space object takes around a star, planet, or moon.

probe – a spacecraft that explores outer space without people onboard.

satellite – an object that orbits, or goes around, a planet.

INDEX

drag, 20–21, 29

engines, 10, 13–14, 28–29

fuel, 10, 13–14, 28–29

gravity, 9, 29

launching, 4, 7, 9, 16

nose cones, 22

orbit, 4, 7, 9, 14, 29

Space Launch System (SLS), 29

stages, 13–15

thrust, 9, 10, 28–29

ONLINE RESOURCES
popbooksonline.com

Scan this code* and others like it while you read, or visit the website below to make this book pop!

popbooksonline.com/rocket-challenge

*Scanning QR codes requires a web-enabled smart device with a QR code reader app and a camera.